W9-ARU-757

Series 633

Here is a book which provides 24 safe and fascinating answers to the question children ask on occasions—"Mummy what can I do?"

It suggests how children can be kept happily and rewardingly occupied for many hours, using simple, inexpensive and readily available materials. Even a convalescent child in bed will be able to make some of the objects.

Teachers, too, will find this a useful book for the younger child.

In the instructions for making each of the objects in this book, it has been suggested that all necessary articles be placed on sheets of old newspaper to avoid making any mess. An old tray might also be useful for holding jars of paint and water.

Where lacquer, paint or clear varnish are required, these should be of the quick-drying variety, which can be obtained in very small quantities from your local model or handicraft shop.

THINGS TO MAKE

by MIA F. RICHEY

with illustrations by
G. ROBINSON

Publishers: Ladybird Books Ltd . Loughborough
© Ladybird Books Ltd (formerly Wills & Hepworth Ltd) 1963
Printed in England

A SEA-SHELL VASE

Would you like to make a vase for Mummy?

THE THINGS YOU WILL NEED:

>An old syrup tin.
>
>Some sea-shells.
>
>Poster paints.
>
>Clear varnish.
>
>Putty.
>
>A paint brush.

PLACE THESE ON SOME
SHEETS OF OLD NEWSPAPER.

WHAT YOU HAVE TO DO :

1. Paint the sea-shells and leave them to dry.

2. Cover the sides of the tin evenly with putty.

3. Push the sea-shells into the putty.

4. When the putty is dry, you can brush over the sea-shells and putty with varnish.

Mummy is sure to like this pretty vase.

0 7214 0125 2

MAKING A TOY SNAKE

*Your young brother or sister will enjoy
pulling this along the ground.*

THE THINGS YOU WILL NEED :

A long piece of string.
10 empty cotton reels.
2 corks.
Green, yellow and black paint or lacquer.
An old rubber ball.
A paint brush.

PLACE THESE ON SOME
SHEETS OF OLD NEWSPAPER.

WHAT YOU HAVE TO DO :

1. Paint the reels and ball green, with yellow spots.

2. Ask Mummy, or Daddy, or your Teacher to make holes for the string through the ball and corks.

3. Paint the corks black.

4. Paint two eyes on the ball, which is the snake's head.

5. Tie a knot at the end of the string, and thread the other end through one of the corks.

6. Thread the reels on to the string; then the ball, and then the other cork.

A PICTURE FOR YOUR ROOM

Have you a picture to frame?

THE THINGS YOU WILL NEED :

A pretty picture.

A round cheese-spread box.

Glue.

Poster paint and a brush.

A piece of ribbon.

Scissors.

PLACE THESE ON SOME
SHEETS OF OLD NEWSPAPER.

WHAT YOU HAVE TO DO :

1. Cut a large circle out of the box lid, leaving a narrow edging.

2. Paint the outside of both halves of the box.

3. Stick the picture inside the bottom of the box.

4. Glue the lid on to the box.

5. Make a bow with ribbon and stick it on the back of the box, making sure you have the picture the right way up.

Now you can hang your picture on the wall.

MAKING A WHIP AND TOP

This will be fun to play with.

THE THINGS YOU WILL NEED :

An empty cotton reel.

A round stick about 15 inches long.
(This is called a dowel rod).

A round stick about $2\frac{1}{2}$ inches long; this
must be the right thickness to fit through
the hole in the reel.
(A wooden meat skewer will often fit).

Paint and a brush.

A penknife and some strong string.

PLACE THESE ON SOME
SHEETS OF OLD NEWSPAPER.

WHAT YOU HAVE TO DO :

1. Sharpen one end of the $2\frac{1}{2}$ inch rod.

2. Push this through the reel so that the point
   sticks well out at the bottom. The rod must be
   a tight fit. This is your top, and you can paint
   it any colour you like.

3. Make a small groove near the end of the longer
   stick. Tie the string tightly in this groove, this
   is your whip.

See how long you can keep your top spinning.

THE CHILDREN IN THE SHOE

This would make a nice present for a little girl.

THE THINGS YOU WILL NEED :

An old shoe (ask Mummy which shoe you may have).

Coloured paints or lacquer and a brush.

Some tiny dolls.

Some scraps of old material, and piece of old ribbon.

PLACE THESE ON SOME
SHEETS OF OLD NEWSPAPER.

WHAT YOU HAVE TO DO :

1. Scrub the shoe and dry it well.

2. Paint it yellow.

3. Paint a window at the toe and one at the heel.

4. Paint flowers and grass along the bottom.

5. If the shoe has lace holes, you could thread ribbon through them.

6. Make some skirts for your dolls, using the ribbon for shoulder straps.

These are the children who lived in a shoe.

A DECORATED PLATE

*If you take care with this it will look
nice in your living room.*

THE THINGS YOU WILL NEED :

An old white dinner plate.
Some glue.
A few old magazines.
Enamel or oil paint (a bright colour).
A brush and some scissors.
A small piece of sponge.

PLACE THESE ON SOME SHEETS OF OLD
NEWSPAPER. STAND THE PAINT POT ON AN
OLD TRAY IF POSSIBLE.

WHAT YOU HAVE TO DO :

1. Cut pictures of objects from the magazines,
   such as a jug or vase, some flowers, a bunch of
   grapes, or other fruits.
2. Arrange some of these to form a nice picture
   in the middle of the plate.
3. Stick them in position carefully.
4. Paint the plate all round the picture, stopping
   half-an-inch from the edges of the picture.
5. Dab round the edge of the paint with a piece
   of sponge, so that it blurs the edge.
6. Allow the paint to dry well. You can then
   varnish your plate if you wish.

*You can stand your plate on a shelf
or hang it on a wall.*

A COLOURFUL WHIRR

You can have great fun with this toy.

THE THINGS YOU WILL NEED :

A piece of cardboard, about 5 inches long and 2 inches wide.

3 feet 6 inches of strong string.

A knitting needle to bore holes.

A pencil and a ruler.

Crayons.

PLACE THESE ON SOME
SHEETS OF OLD NEWSPAPER.

WHAT YOU HAVE TO DO :

1. Using your ruler, draw lines from corner to corner of the cardboard.
2. Bore holes close to the centre as shown.
3. Draw coloured stripes on both sides of the cardboard.
4. Thread the end of the string through one hole, then back through the other hole.
5. Tie the ends of the string together, and pull the string until the whirr is in centre.

This is your new toy. Have fun whirring it!

AN INDIAN HEAD-DRESS

*You will enjoy making this—**and** playing with it.*

THE THINGS YOU WILL NEED :

A piece of corrugated cardboard, about 3 feet long.

Some wide cellotape.

Some long feathers.

Scissors.

Coloured inks.

Two paper clips.

PLACE THESE ON SOME SHEETS OF OLD NEWSPAPER, WITH THE COLOURED INKS ON AN OLD TRAY.

WHAT YOU HAVE TO DO :

1. Colour your feathers and let them dry.

2. Cut corrugated cardboard 1½ inches wide and about 3 feet long.

3. Stick a feather in every sixth hole in the corrugated cardboard.

4. Set the cardboard flat on the table, and put cellotape right along the back over the cardboard and the bottom of the feathers, to hold the feathers in place.

5. Fold the head-dress once in the middle, and then fasten the ends together with a paper clip. Place another paper clip about 10 inches from the fold.

Now you can open it out and put it on, and you are a fine Indian chief.

A WONDERFUL DIVER

You will enjoy making this.

THE THINGS YOU WILL NEED :

A rubber tube from inside an old fountain pen.

A large, clear bottle.

A cork to fit the bottle neck.

A small piece of wire, not *too* thin.

A medium sized knitting needle.

PLACE THESE ON SOME
SHEETS OF OLD NEWSPAPER.

WHAT YOU HAVE TO DO :

1. Cut the tube from the pen. You will now have one open and one closed end.
2. Insert the needle in the open end, but be careful not to push it through the rubber.
3. Wrap the wire tightly round the bottom (open) end of the tube two or three times, and then pull the needle out. Cut off any extra wire. This is your diver.
4. Fill bottle with water up to about an inch from the top. Put the diver in.
5. If the top of the diver is more than $\frac{3}{4}$ of an inch above the water, squeeze his head until a small bubble comes out at the bottom.

Now each time you press the cork in the bottle, the diver will sink to the bottom. When you loosen the cork, it will come to the top again.

A LEATHER SUCKER

This is a toy that boys and girls used to make long ago.

THE THINGS YOU WILL NEED :

A piece of strong leather.

A thin knitting needle for boring hole.

3 feet of strong string of the same thickness as the needle.

Scissors.

An old cup, and a pencil.

PLACE THESE ON A NEWSPAPER.

WHAT YOU HAVE TO DO :

1. Place the cup upside down on the leather and trace round it.

2. Remove the cup and cut out the circle of leather.

3. Bore a hole in the centre with your needle.

4. Thread the string through the hole, and tie a knot at one end so that it will not pull through the hole.

5. Soak your sucker in water until it is quite soft.

Now you can press your sucker tightly against a flat surface—a box for instance, and lift it up by pulling the string.

BOOK ENDS OR DOOR STOPS

These will make a very useful present for adults.

THE THINGS YOU WILL NEED :

Plenty of raffia or cord of an even thickness.

Two tins, either round or rectangular (such as syrup or cocoa tins).

Clear varnish and a brush.

Sand.

Scissors.

Red paint and lacquer.

PLACE THESE ON SOME SHEETS OF OLD NEWSPAPER, WITH THE VARNISH AND PAINT ON AN OLD TRAY.

WHAT YOU HAVE TO DO :

1. Fill both tins with sand, and put the lids on tightly.

2. Paint the lids and bottoms of the tins red.

3. Plait raffia or cord in long strands.

4. Varnish the tins and allow them to become slightly sticky.

5. Wrap the plaits evenly round the sides of the tins (taking care to keep your fingers off the varnish). When you have covered the sides, tuck the ends well in.

6. Varnish the plaits and allow them to dry.

There! Mummy and Daddy will be pleased!

A FLOWERPOT HOLDER

This will look most attractive.

THE THINGS YOU WILL NEED :

A small flowerpot.
A jar of vaseline.
Wallpaper paste.
Some newspaper.
Paints, clear varnish and brushes.

PLACE THESE ON SOME
SHEETS OF OLD NEWSPAPER.

WHAT YOU HAVE TO DO :

1. Grease the outside of the flowerpot with vaseline.
2. Tear the newspaper into tiny pieces about the size of a stamp.
3. Turn the pot upside down.
4. Stick the pieces of newspaper over the pot until it is well covered.
5. Paste over this paper, then stick on another layer of paper and let it dry.
6. Paste all over again and stick on more paper.
7. Keep doing this until you have about seven layers of paper on the pot.
8. Let it dry well, and then slide out the pot.
9. Paint the flowerpot holder, and varnish it when the paint is dry.

Now you have a very nice holder for Mummy to put her flowerpot in.

A FALSE FACE

This is a strong mask which should give you lots of fun.

THE THINGS YOU WILL NEED :

> A cereal box.
> Cotton wool.
> About 12 inches of elastic.
> Glue and scissors.
> Poster paints and brush.

PLACE THESE ON SOME
SHEETS OF OLD NEWSPAPER.

WHAT YOU HAVE TO DO :

1. Cut off the back and bottom of the box, so that you have the top and three sides left.
2. Paint the outside of the box. Pale pink would be a good colour.
3. Cut holes for the eyes and mouth.
4. Attach the elastic to the sides across the open back, to hold the face on.
5. Glue cotton wool on the top and sides (this is your hair).
6. Paint a nose and lips. If you wish, you can now glue on cotton wool eyebrows and a moustache.

*Your friends will laugh when they see
you in this strange disguise.*

A USEFUL HEARTH BRUSH

Here is another acceptable little present.

THE THINGS YOU WILL NEED :

2 feet of thick rope (about $\frac{1}{2}$ an inch in diameter).

Some raffia or raffine.

About 18 inches of strong string.

Clear varnish.

An old comb.

PLACE THESE ON SOME
SHEETS OF OLD NEWSPAPER.

WHAT YOU HAVE TO DO :

1. Double the rope.

2. Bind it tightly with string about 4 inches from the bottom. Use half your string for this, then cut it and tie a knot—tucking the knot neatly into the rope. Bind again about 3 inches from the loop, again tucking in the knot.

3. Bind the raffia evenly round the rope, and over and between the two pieces of string. Keep it flat and overlapping, so that the rope does not show through it.

4. Unwind the bottom 4 inches of rope and comb it out. This makes the bristles of your brush.

5. Varnish your brush except the bristles.

A NECKLACE OF PAPER BEADS

Ask Daddy if he has any scraps of wallpaper which you can have. Here is a way to use them.

THE THINGS YOU WILL NEED :

      Brightly coloured wallpaper.

      A fine knitting needle.

      Some wallpaper paste and a brush.

      About 30 inches of thin string.

      Clear varnish.

      Scissors.

PLACE THESE ON SOME
SHEETS OF OLD NEWSPAPER.

WHAT YOU HAVE TO DO :

1. Cut the paper into strips about 8 inches long and $\frac{1}{2}$ an inch wide.

2. Paste the backs of the strips.

3. Roll each strip firmly round the needle. Press firmly, then take it off the needle and let it dry. You will need to make quite a lot for a necklace.

4. Now varnish your beads.

5. Thread them on the string, and knot the ends of the string together.

You will look nice wearing these !

A MINIATURE GARDEN

This will look lovely on the window-ledge.

THE THINGS YOU WILL NEED :

A bowl (or similar container).

A broken plant pot.

Some fine soil or, better still, potting compost.

Small white stones.

A mirror.

Some rockery plants.

PLACE THESE ON SOME
SHEETS OF OLD NEWSPAPER.

WHAT YOU HAVE TO DO :

1. Break the plant pot into small pieces, and place these at the bottom of the bowl.

2. Fill the bowl with fine soil (or potting compost) up to 1 inch from the top.

3. Place the mirror on the soil (this makes a fine pond).

4. Make a path with the small stones, leading to and around the pond.

5. Set in your rockery plants. Not too many, because these will spread as they grow.

Now you have a miniature garden of your own, you must water it two or three times a week (just enough to keep the soil moist), and make sure it gets some sunshine.

A PAIR OF STILTS

Would you like to be 5 inches taller?

THE THINGS YOU WILL NEED :

> 2 syrup tins.
>
> A nail (for punching holes).
>
> 2 long pieces of string.
>
> Some paint or lacquer and a brush.

PLACE THESE ON SOME
SHEETS OF OLD NEWSPAPER.

WHAT YOU HAVE TO DO :

1. Punch a hole at each side of both tins, near the bottom.

2. If you wish, you can paint the tins, and leave them to dry.

3. Thread a piece of string through both holes of one tin, and tie the ends together so that the knot is inside the tin. Do the same with the other tin.

4. The string should be long enough for you to hold it while standing up straight on the bottoms of the tins.

Now you can try walking on your stilts.

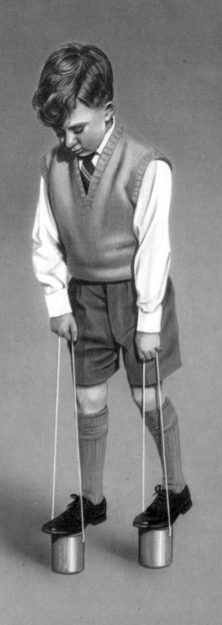

A COLOURFUL MOBILE

This makes a pretty decoration.

THE THINGS YOU WILL NEED :

A wire coathanger.
Some strong cotton.
Some egg shell halves.
Old nail varnish or coloured lacquer.
Christmas frost or glitter.
A brush.
A darning needle.

PLACE THESE ON SOME
SHEETS OF OLD NEWSPAPER.

WHAT YOU HAVE TO DO :

1. Make a small hole in the top of each egg shell with the needle.

2. Cut the cotton in different lengths, then knot one end of each piece and thread through a shell so that the knot is on the inside.

3. Lacquer the shells in different colours, and sprinkle with glitter while they are wet.

4. When they are dry, hang them from the coat-hanger with the cotton.

Now you can hang your mobile in a good draught and watch it move.

PATTERN PRINTING WITH A POTATO

You will have fun making potato prints.

THE THINGS YOU WILL NEED :

A medium-sized potato.

A knife. Ask Mummy for one that is not too sharp.

Some thick poster paint in a flat dish.

Drawing paper or the back of old wallpaper.

PLACE THESE ON SOME SHEETS OF OLD NEWSPAPER, ON A GOOD FLAT SURFACE.

WHAT YOU HAVE TO DO :

1. Wash and dry your potato.
2. Cut it in half.
3. On one half draw an easy shape—a square or perhaps a cross.
4. Shade the drawing lightly with paint.
5. Cut away the part not shaded, so that the pattern shape stands higher than the rest.
6. Press the raised shape in the paint.
7. Now press the potato carefully on the paper. You should get two or three copies of your shape before dipping it in the paint again.

When you have had some practice, you can try all sorts of shapes to print, and make lovely patterns.

INVISIBLE INK FOR SECRET MESSAGES

Here is another surprise for your friends.

THE THINGS YOU WILL NEED :

> One onion.
>
> An empty ink or other small bottle.
>
> A pen.
>
> A small bowl.
>
> Some writing paper.

PLACE THESE ON SOME
SHEETS OF OLD NEWSPAPER.

WHAT YOU HAVE TO DO :

1. Cut the onion in half, and squeeze the juice into the bowl.
2. Pour the juice into your bottle. It will look just like water.
3. Using this juice as ink, write a message on the paper.
4. Allow it to dry slowly by itself.

Now you can astonish your friends by holding the paper close to the heat from a lamp, and your message will appear.

NOW TRY CLAY MODELLING

There are many different kinds of clay for modelling, but this is the cleanest.

THE THINGS YOU WILL NEED :

A large bowl or basin.

2 cups of plain flour.

1 cup of salt.

1 tablespoonful of powdered alum (you can get this from a chemist).

About 1 cup of water.

PLACE THESE ON AN OLD TRAY, AND PUT THE TRAY ON SOME SHEETS OF OLD NEWSPAPER.

WHAT YOU HAVE TO DO :

1. Mix the flour, salt and alum together in the bowl.
2. Add water in small quantities, and mix it well until it is firm enough for modelling. Be careful not to make it too wet.
3. Now you may start modelling, and you can let your shapes harden if you wish.
4. This clay can be coloured with dyes, inks or cake colouring.
5. If you are not using your clay, keep it in an airtight jar.

You can make ashtrays, animal models and lots of other things. Once a boy made a model farmyard. Perhaps you could make one ?

A CHRISTMAS LOG

This will make a lovely Christmas present.

THE THINGS YOU WILL NEED :

A good thick log about 7 inches long.
White paint or lacquer and a brush.
A sprig of holly and a packet of glitter.
Some drawing pins.
A red candle and some green ribbon.
A piece of thin white card and some glue.
Cotton wool.

PLACE THESE ON SOME
SHEETS OF OLD NEWSPAPER.

WHAT YOU HAVE TO DO :

1. Ask Daddy if he will bore a hole (for the candle) half way through the log, making sure the log sits steadily with the hole at the top.
2. Paint the holly leaves white, and sprinkle them with glitter.
3. Paint white streaks along the log, and sprinkle them with glitter.
4. Paint the heads of drawing pins white, and sprinkle them with glitter also.
5. When the holly and pins are dry, pin the holly to the log.
6. Put the candle in the hole, and with your ribbon tie a bow round the end of the log.
7. Cut an oval shape from the white card, and stick it to the bottom of the log. This will help the log to stand more steadily.
8. Now arrange some cotton wool as you see in the picture.

A DAINTY FAIRY TREE

This will look pretty in the window.

THE THINGS YOU WILL NEED :

A branch with several small twigs on it.

A small flowerpot.

Coloured paint and a brush.

Some small fir cones.

Some pieces of cotton.

Clay, putty or Plasticine.

PLACE THESE ON SOME
SHEETS OF OLD NEWSPAPER.

WHAT YOU HAVE TO DO :

1. Paint the cones in different colours. You can sprinkle them with glitter if you wish.

2. Fill the flowerpot with clay or putty.

3. Plant your tree in the clay.

4. Hang the cones from the twigs with the cotton.

Everyone will say how nice this looks.

A SNOWMAN ON A LAKE

This should look pretty on the Christmas dinner table.

THE THINGS YOU WILL NEED :

> An empty 1 lb. jam jar.
> A potato to sit in the neck of the jar.
> Paste or glue.
> Cotton wool.
> Christmas frost or glitter
> A mirror—not too large.
> Some black paper.
> A strip of material.

PLACE THESE ON SOME
SHEETS OF OLD NEWSPAPER.

WHAT YOU HAVE TO DO :

1. Cover the potato with glue, and then with cotton wool. This is the snowman's head.
2. Cut off a piece of cotton wool big enough to go round the jam jar, and tie a piece of cotton round the neck to keep it in place. Glue to the jar where the ends meet.
3. Set the head on the body, and make an extra collar of cotton wool.
4. Tie the strip of material round the neck for a scarf.
5. Cut small circles from the black paper for the snowman's eyes and buttons, and stick them on. Also make him a mouth.
6. Streak the mirror with glue, and sprinkle frost on it. This is your frozen lake.
7. Set the snowman on the lake.